Medical milestones

Medicine involves learning how the body works, in order to fix parts that aren't working. It's come a long way in a few thousand years!

Smallpox vaccine
British scientist Edward Jenner vaccinates a boy and stops him from getting smallpox.

Ophthalmoscope
German physicist Hermann von Helmholtz invents a device for looking inside the eye.

Thermometer
British physician Thomas Allbutt invents the thermometer to check patients' temperatures.

Thermometers check if you are too hot.

Continued at back of book

| 1796 | 1818 | 1847 | 1851 | 1861 | 1866 | 1867 |

Blood transfusion
British doctor James Blundell replaces lost blood in a patient.

Keeping clean
Hungarian physician Ignaz Semmelweis tells surgeons to wash their hands and surgical instruments properly to help stop the spread of disease.

Speech in the brain
French physician Pierre Paul Broca finds the area of the brain that controls speech.

Washing hands gets rid of bacteria.

Germs
French chemist Louis Pasteur discovers germs and links them with diseases.

Editors Kathleen Teece,
Kritika Gupta
Designer Emma Hobson
Design assistant Bettina Myklebust Stovne
Project art editor Yamini Panwar
DTP designers Ashok Kumar, Dheeraj Singh
Managing editors Laura Gilbert,
Monica Saigal
Managing art editors Diane Peyton Jones,
Neha Ahuja Chowdhry
Jacket co-ordinator Francesca Young
Jacket designer Amy Keast
Picture researcher Sakshi Saluja
Pre-production producer Marina Hartung
Producer Isabell Schart
Art director Martin Wilson
Publisher Sarah Larter
Publishing director Sophie Mitchell
Educational consultant Jacqueline Harris

First published in Great Britain in 2017 by
Dorling Kindersley Limited
80 Strand, London, WC2R 0RL

Copyright © 2017 Dorling Kindersley Limited
A Penguin Random House Company
10 9 8 7 6 5 4 3 2 1
001–299030–Sep/2017

A CIP catalogue record for this book
is available from the British Library.
ISBN: 978-0-2412-8507-7

Printed and bound in China

A WORLD OF IDEAS:
SEE ALL THERE IS TO KNOW

www.dk.com

Contents

4   Inside out

6   Growth

8   The bare bones

10   The skull

12   The brain

14   Nervous system

16   Muscle power

18   Organs

20   Heart to heart

22   Breathing

24   Blood

Fetus

Brain

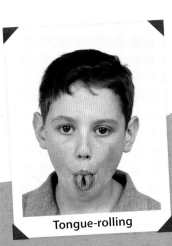

Tongue-rolling

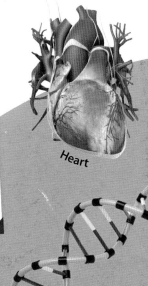

Heart

26 Immune squad

28 Healing

30 Digestion

32 Getting energy

34 Teeth

36 The body clock

38 Genes

40 Senses

42 Eyes

44 Hearing

46 Taste and smell

48 Emotions

50 Skin bacteria

52 Bacteria... or virus?

54 Exercise

56 Superhuman

58 Human body facts and figures

60 Glossary

62 Index

64 Acknowledgements

Tooth

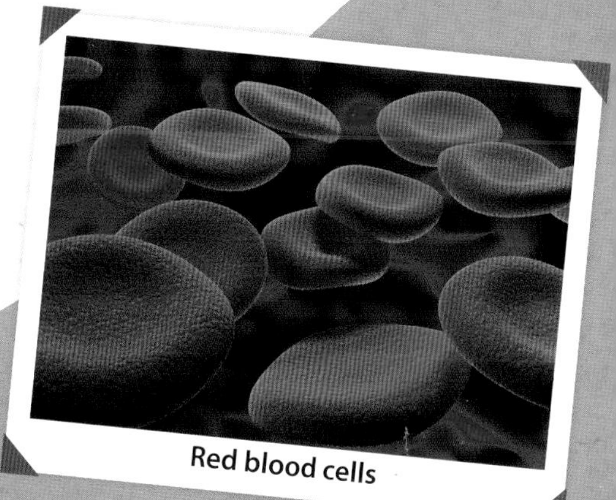

Stomach

Muscles

Red blood cells

DNA

Skull

3

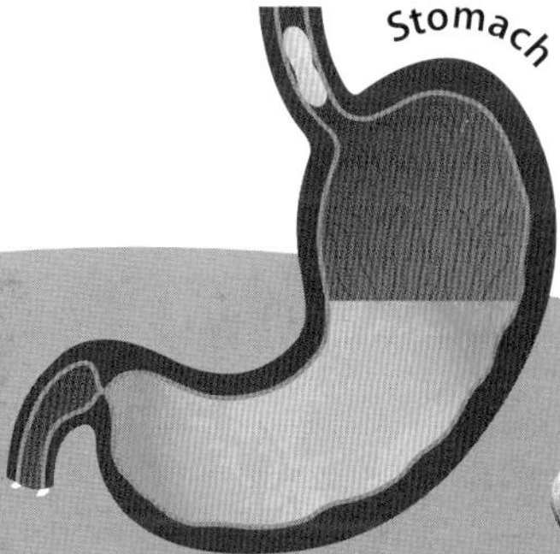

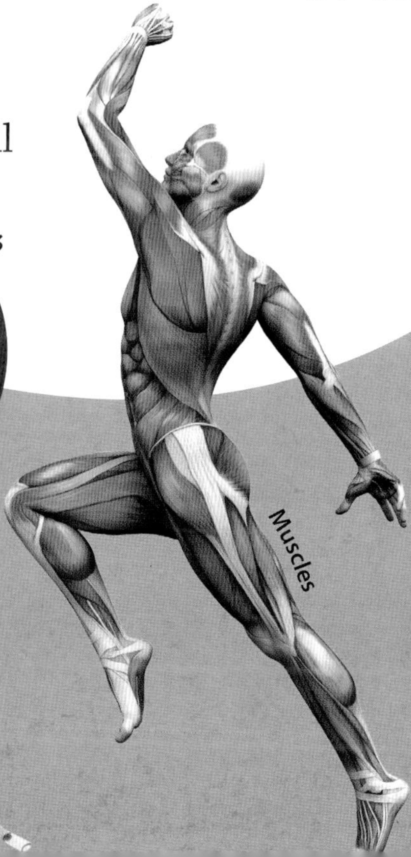

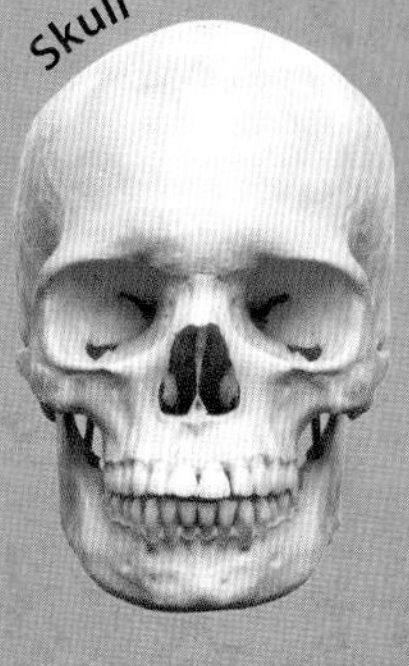

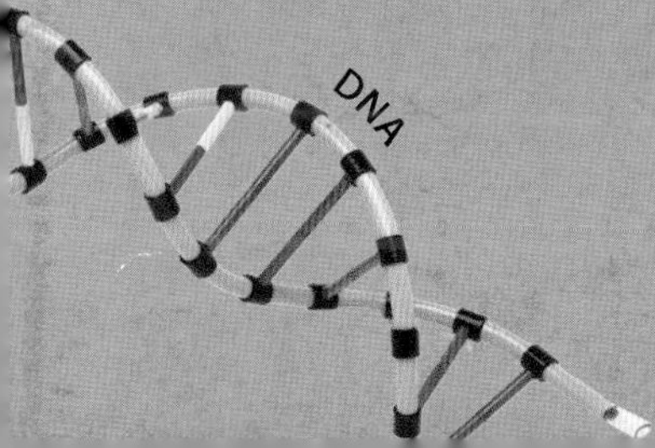

The cell
The cell is the smallest living part of the body. Different cells do different jobs.

Tissues
Similar cells form tissues. There are four tissue types in the body, including muscle tissue.

Tissues in the liver do similar jobs, like get rid of poisons in food.

Inside out

The body is made up of 300 bones, 24 organs, 11 organ systems, and at least 8 m (26 ft) of bowel! The brain controls everything to help them work together. The skin is a strong waterproof wrapping paper that keeps the body together in a neat shape.

Organs
Similar tissues join together to form organs, like the heart and kidneys.

Organ system

Organs that carry out similar jobs make up organ systems such as the digestive system.

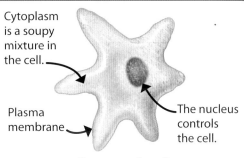

Digestive organs help break down food for the body.

The body

The different organ systems join together to make one individual human being like you!

The cell

Cells are made up of even tinier structures that work to help the cell do its job. The plasma membrane surrounds each cell. It is like a fence that controls what comes into the cell.

Cytoplasm is a soupy mixture in the cell.

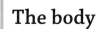

Plasma membrane

The nucleus controls the cell.

Structure of a cell

Growth

Bones start to form at around six weeks old in the womb and continue to grow into adulthood. As bones become longer, muscles grow and get stronger. Organs get bigger and we get heavier.

12 years old
Bones continue to grow so the child gets taller. They should exercise to make their bones stronger.

Embryo
Life begins as a ball of cells called an embryo in the mother's womb. The cells divide so that there are more cells to form a fetus.

Infant
Babies usually start to walk at around the age of one. Many of their bones are very soft.

Bone cells harden into strong bones.

The fetus is curled up in the womb.

A six-week-old embryo is around 5 mm ($^2/_{25}$ in) long.

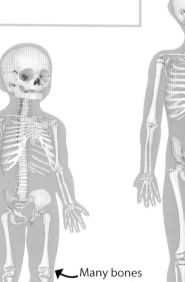

Many bones join together as infants age.

Fetus
It takes nine months to grow a baby. While it is in the mother's womb, it is called a fetus.

Four years old
Most of the soft bones from infancy have hardened by the age of four.

Hormones tell the bones to keep growing.

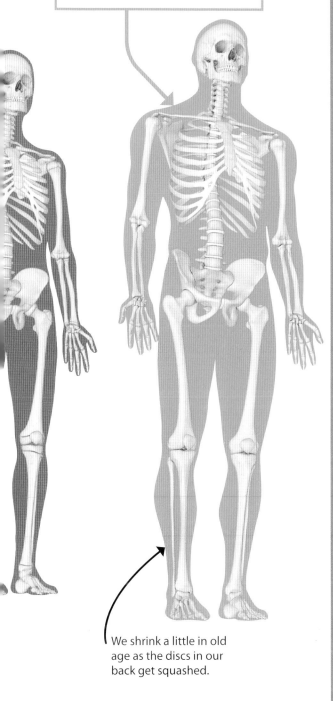

Adult

An adult is fully grown from around the age of 18. This means their bones will not grow any longer.

We shrink a little in old age as the discs in our back get squashed.

Bone shapes

We have different shapes of bone that help us to move in different ways. Each shape is made to match the job of the bone in the body. Small bones allow lots of movement. Other bones are made to support us and give us strength.

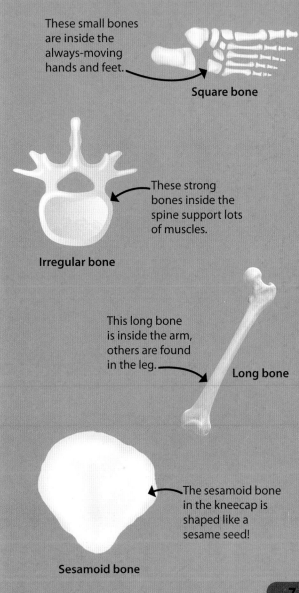

These small bones are inside the always-moving hands and feet.

Square bone

These strong bones inside the spine support lots of muscles.

Irregular bone

This long bone is inside the arm, others are found in the leg.

Long bone

The sesamoid bone in the kneecap is shaped like a sesame seed!

Sesamoid bone

The bare bones

Bones keep your body parts together and hold everything upright. They protect soft organs, such as the heart. Bones store calcium, which is needed for important jobs in the body. Marrow inside a bone makes new red blood cells, which take oxygen to our body parts. Muscles pull on bones to make you move.

X-ray

X-ray photos show bones through the skin. A doctor will take an X-ray if they think you have broken a bone.

X-rays show bones in white because they are the most solid bits.

Spine

This column that runs up your back is made up of 33 bones. It protects the spinal cord connecting the body and brain.

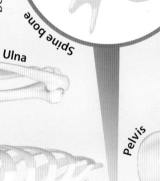

Spine bone

Cartilage

Squishy cartilage connects bones together that need to move, such as ribs for breathing.

Cartilage in blue surrounded by other tissue.

Inside cartilage

Skull

Clavicle

Carpals

Ulna

Pelvis

Spine

Ribs

Humerus

Radius

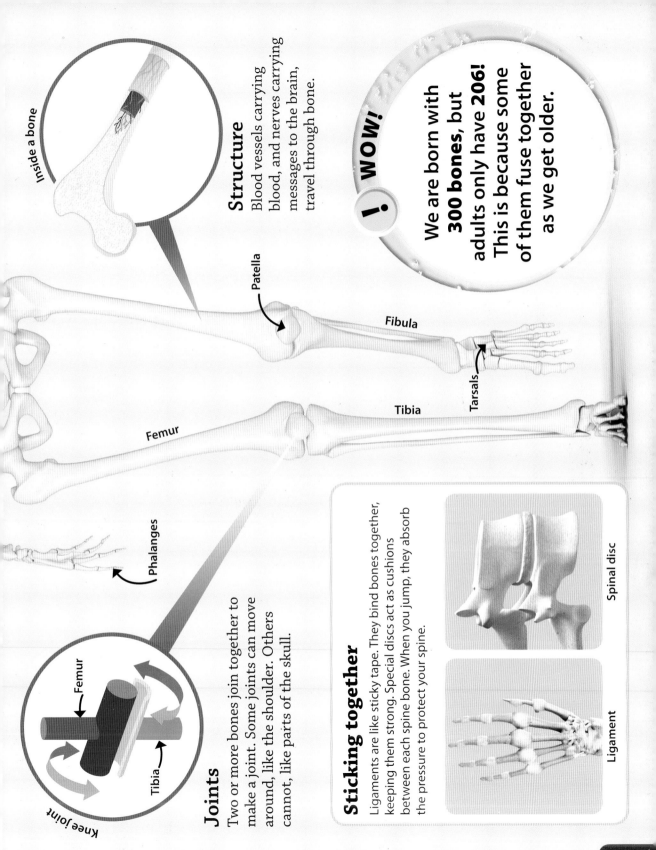

Inside a bone

Structure

Blood vessels carrying blood, and nerves carrying messages to the brain, travel through bone.

Patella

Fibula

Tarsals

Tibia

Femur

Phalanges

Joints

Two or more bones join together to make a joint. Some joints can move around, like the shoulder. Others cannot, like parts of the skull.

Femur

Tibia

Knee joint

Sticking together

Ligaments are like sticky tape. They bind bones together, keeping them strong. Special discs act as cushions between each spine bone. When you jump, they absorb the pressure to protect your spine.

Spinal disc

Ligament

The skull

It might look like one big lump of bone, but more than 20 different bones make up your skull. It is an amazing structure that keeps the brain, eyes, and ears safe. The bones are very tough, so if you bump your head, the skull keeps your squishy brain nice and safe.

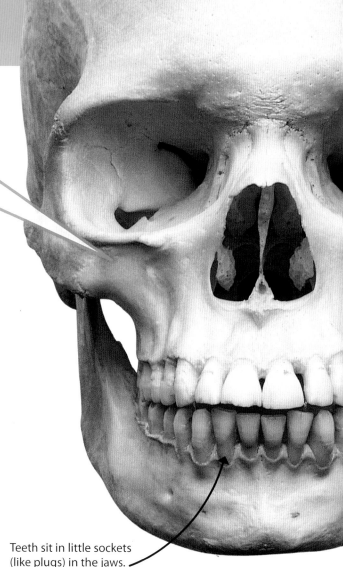

Upper jaw
You can feel the inside of the upper jaw by touching the roof of your mouth.

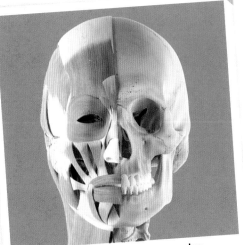

We have more than 20 muscles attached to the skull bones. These help us to smile, pull faces, and eat.

Teeth sit in little sockets (like plugs) in the jaws.

Cranium

This is the brain box. It is tough and strong and made up of eight bones. It is like a protective helmet for the brain.

Tunnels carry sounds from the ears to the brain.

Six tiny muscles attached to the eye sockets move the eyeballs around.

! WOW!

Tiny holes in the skull let **blood vessels** and **nerves** reach the brain.

Lower jaw

You can chew food because the lower jaw can move, unlike any other part of the skull. Muscles contract (shorten) to move the jaw.

Growth of skull

The shape and size of the skull changes as we get older. As our brains grow, the skull bones also have to grow. A baby's skull is very soft because it has to be as small and flexible as possible during birth. The bones harden over time to form a tough adult skull.

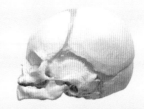

Newborn skull
The skull bones are separate and can slide over one another during birth.

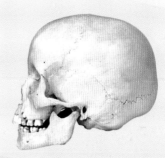

Six-year-old skull
As the brain has stopped growing, the skull bones start to join up.

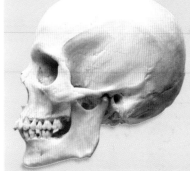

Adult skull
The brain and skull have stopped growing. The bones are joined together to form a strong box around the brain.

The brain

The brain is the control centre of your body. This wrinkly organ controls everything you do, from breathing to recognizing your friends' faces. It is full of electrical connections that tell you how to understand language, how to do maths, and how to use your imagination.

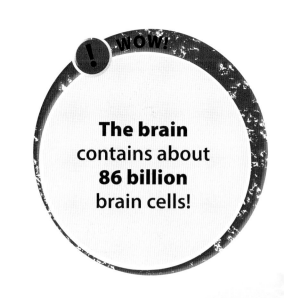

WOW!

The brain contains about **86 billion** brain cells!

Left and right side

The right half of the brain controls the left side of the body, and the left half controls your right side. Both sides of the brain are connected by a thick band of fibres.

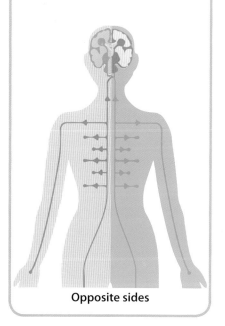

Opposite sides

Happiness

Personality

The front part of your brain controls many things, including your personality. It is called the frontal lobe.

Sound

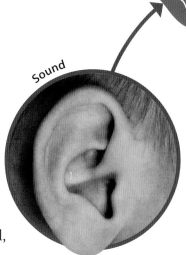

Hearing

Sounds we hear are worked out in this part of the brain, so we can tell if they are loud, soft, or squeaky.

Jumping

Moving

Instructions that tell your muscles what to do come from an area called the motor cortex in the frontal lobe.

Spatial awareness

What's around

This part of the brain makes you aware of where your body is in relation to things around you. This is called spatial awareness.

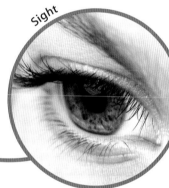

Sight

Seeing

The optic nerve brings sight information from the eyes to this area. It is called the occipital (ocks-ih-PIT-al) lobe.

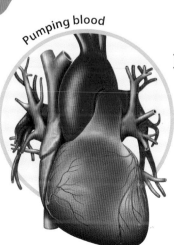

Pumping blood

Heartbeat

The brainstem joins the brain to the spinal cord, which carries instructions to your body. Your heart is controlled here.

Nervous system

The brain has lots of electrical connections with the rest of the body. These connections are called nerves. They carry messages to and from the brain. The brain tells our body parts to move, and the body tells the brain what is happening around us. We have too many nerves to count!

Brain
Nerves tell the brain what we can see and hear, as well as other information.

Spinal cord
Nerves that come off the spinal cord are called spinal nerves. They travel around the whole body.

Movement
Nerves carry instructions from the brain to the body's muscles to tell them when and how hard to work.

Stomach muscles
Nerves tell these muscles to bend your body to touch your toes.

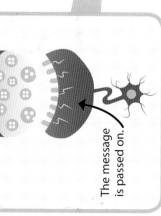

Neurotransmitters are released from a nerve.

The message is passed on.

Nerve messengers
Chemical messengers, called neurotransmitters, pass on information from the end of one nerve to the beginning of another.

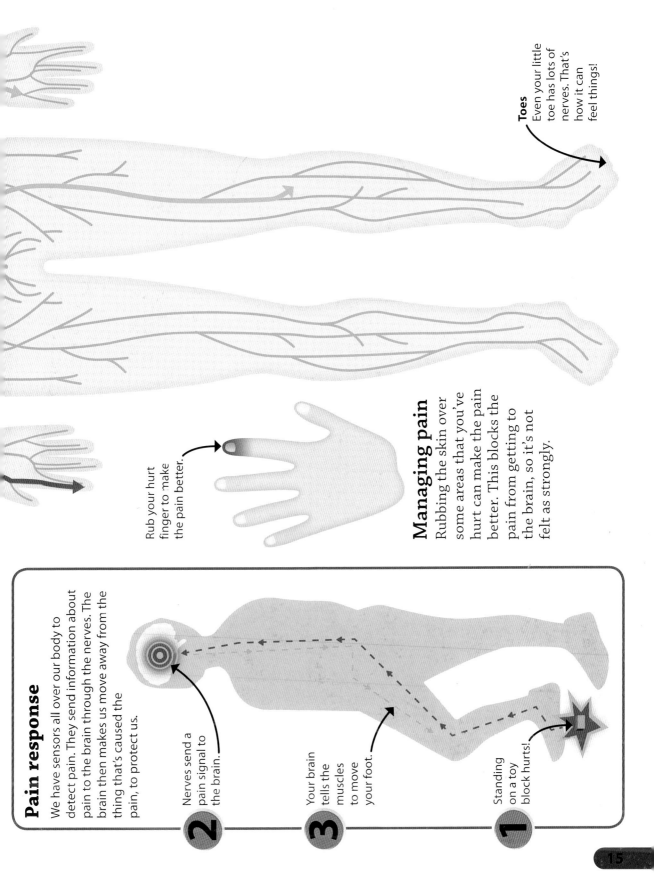

Toes
Even your little toe has lots of nerves. That's how it can feel things!

Rub your hurt finger to make the pain better.

Managing pain

Rubbing the skin over some areas that you've hurt can make the pain better. This blocks the pain from getting to the brain, so it's not felt as strongly.

Pain response

We have sensors all over our body to detect pain. They send information about pain to the brain through the nerves. The brain then makes us move away from the thing that's caused the pain, to protect us.

2 Nerves send a pain signal to the brain.

3 Your brain tells the muscles to move your foot.

1 Standing on a toy block hurts!

Muscle power

You used muscles in your hands to turn this page over. Muscles contract (shorten) to cause movement. They are attached to your bones, and pull on them to make your body parts move. Muscles inside you push food through the digestive system, and blood around your body.

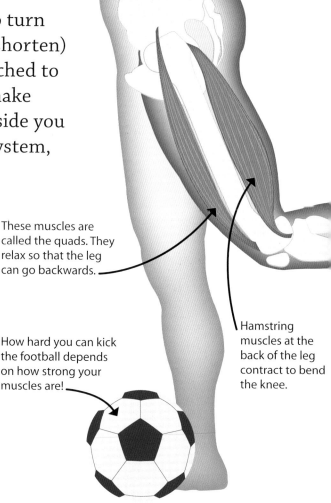

These muscles are called the quads. They relax so that the leg can go backwards.

Hamstring muscles at the back of the leg contract to bend the knee.

How hard you can kick the football depends on how strong your muscles are!

Muscle pairs

Muscles work together to make smooth movements, whether it's picking up a drink or playing sport. When you raise your leg backwards to kick a football, muscles at the back of your leg contract. At the same time, muscles at the front relax.

Types of muscle

There are three types of muscle in the body called smooth, cardiac, and skeletal. Skeletal muscle contracts when we want it to. Other muscle types have a mind of their own!

Smooth muscle
All blood vessels and most organs have this muscle type. It lines the different tubes that transport blood and food. This muscle contracts whether or not we want it to!

Muscle contracts to squeeze food through the intestinal tubes.

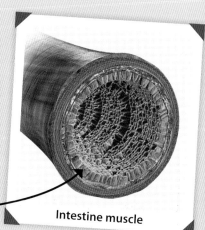

Intestine muscle

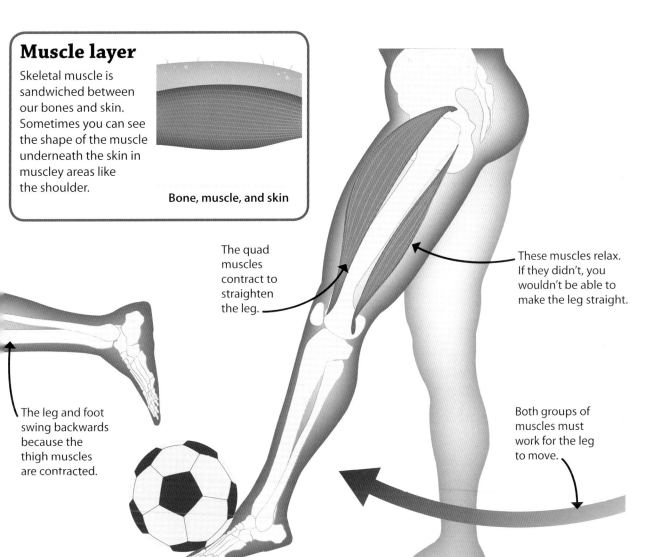

Muscle layer

Skeletal muscle is sandwiched between our bones and skin. Sometimes you can see the shape of the muscle underneath the skin in muscley areas like the shoulder.

Bone, muscle, and skin

The quad muscles contract to straighten the leg.

These muscles relax. If they didn't, you wouldn't be able to make the leg straight.

The leg and foot swing backwards because the thigh muscles are contracted.

Both groups of muscles must work for the leg to move.

Cardiac muscle

Cardiac muscle is only found in the heart. Without you telling it to, it pumps blood into blood vessels and around the body.

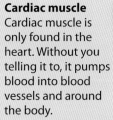

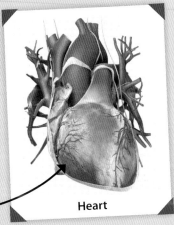

The heart is a big, important bag of muscle.

Heart

Skeletal muscle

You wouldn't be able to pull funny faces without skeletal muscle. It contracts to help you raise your eyebrows or puff out your cheeks.

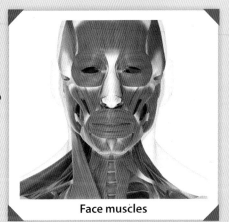

Face muscles

Organs

Each one of the 24 organs in your body has a special job to do. Organs work together to carry out tasks. When you breathe in and out through the nose, you also use your lungs and windpipe. Match the eight organs missing from this body.

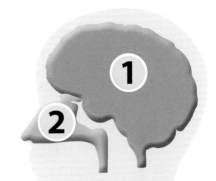

Organ transplant

A transplant is when doctors remove an organ that isn't working properly and replace it with a healthy one.

Transporting a replacement organ.

! WOW!

Skin is the **largest organ** in the human body!

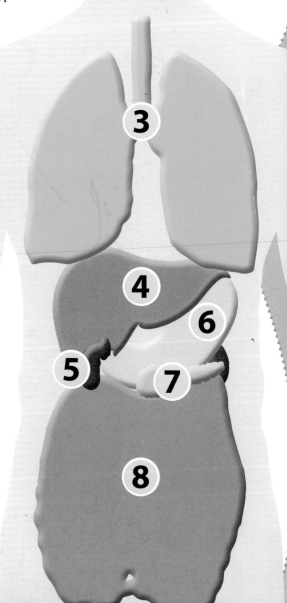

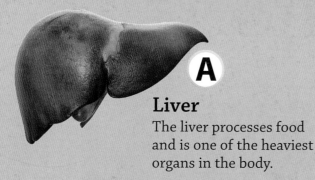

A

Liver
The liver processes food and is one of the heaviest organs in the body.

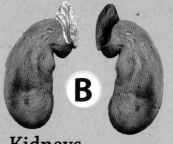

B

Kidneys
These clean the blood to make wee. They connect to the bladder. We have two but can survive with one!

C

Nose
Hairs inside the nose trap dirt to keep our lungs clean when we breathe in. It also sniffs out nasty smells!

D

Stomach
This organ breaks down food using acids that turn food into mush. The stomach stretches when we eat.

E

Pancreas
The pancreas makes juice for breaking down food and keeps blood sugar levels normal.

Bowels
Every last bit of goodness in the food you eat is soaked up by the bowels, before it becomes poo.

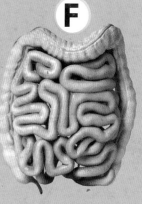

F

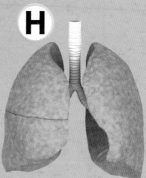

H

G

Brain
This controls everything in the body through electrical connections.

Lungs
The lungs take oxygen from the air and deliver it to the blood. The windpipe joins them together.

Heart to heart

The heart's job is to pump blood around your body. This organ is like a house with two floors, and two rooms in each. Blood is received into the atria at the top of the heart from the lungs and body. It is then passed into the super-strong ventricles at the bottom, and squeezed around the body and to the lungs.

Pumping blood

The heart is a bag of muscle. It squeezes blood to the lungs and the rest of the body through blood vessels. Oxygen in the blood can therefore reach body parts to keep them healthy, and carbon dioxide in the blood can reach the lungs to be breathed out.

Blood vessels
These are tubes that carry blood around the body.

Heart

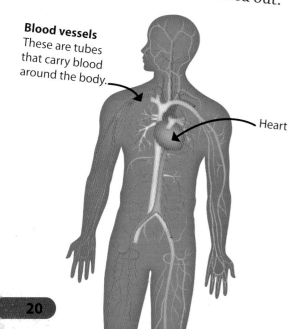

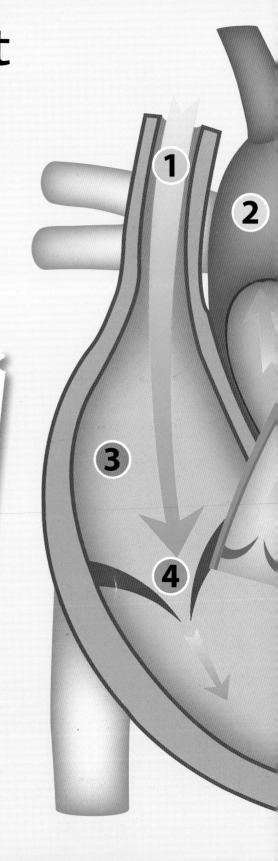

Animal hearts

Animals, including humans, have different sized hearts. The human heart is the size of your fist. A blue whale's heart is bigger than you! Whales have a much larger body to pump blood around.

Blue whale heart

Arteries have thick walls. They can expand as the heart pumps blood through them.

2

3

1

4

These veins carry blood from the lungs to the left atrium.

The heart walls are made of muscle and covered in some fat.

5

5

KEY

» **1. Veins** These blood vessels carry blood back to the heart from the body.

» **2. Arteries** These blood vessels carry blood away from the heart.

» **3. Atria** Each atritum receives blood from the body or lungs, and pumps it into a ventricle.

» **4. Valves** Gate-like structures that let blood flow in one direction only.

» **5. Ventricles** Thick walls let these pump blood to the whole body and lungs.

! WOW!

When it's really cold, your fingers **turn blue** because the **blood vessels** shut down!

Breathing

When we take air into and out of our lungs, we are breathing. This keeps the body's cells alive. Put a hand on your chest and take a deep breath in. You can feel the air go into your lungs as your chest goes up. The organs we use to breathe make up the respiratory system.

Asthma

Respiratory conditions like asthma make it hard to breathe. Tubes for transporting oxygen in the lungs swell inwards and produce mucus, which stops oxygen getting through.

Asthma inhalers calm the airways.

Oxygen and carbon dioxide

These two gases are found in the air that we breathe. Plants take carbon dioxide in and release oxygen into the air. This is the opposite of what humans do!

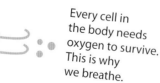

Every cell in the body needs oxygen to survive. This is why we breathe.

Cells make carbon dioxide as a waste product. We breathe this out to remove it.

Blood vessels carry oxygen-filled red blood cells to the rest of the body.

Alveoli

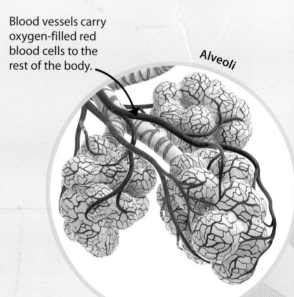

Transporting oxygen

Red blood cells act as delivery trucks. They pick up oxygen from the alveoli and carry it to the body's cells through blood vessels.

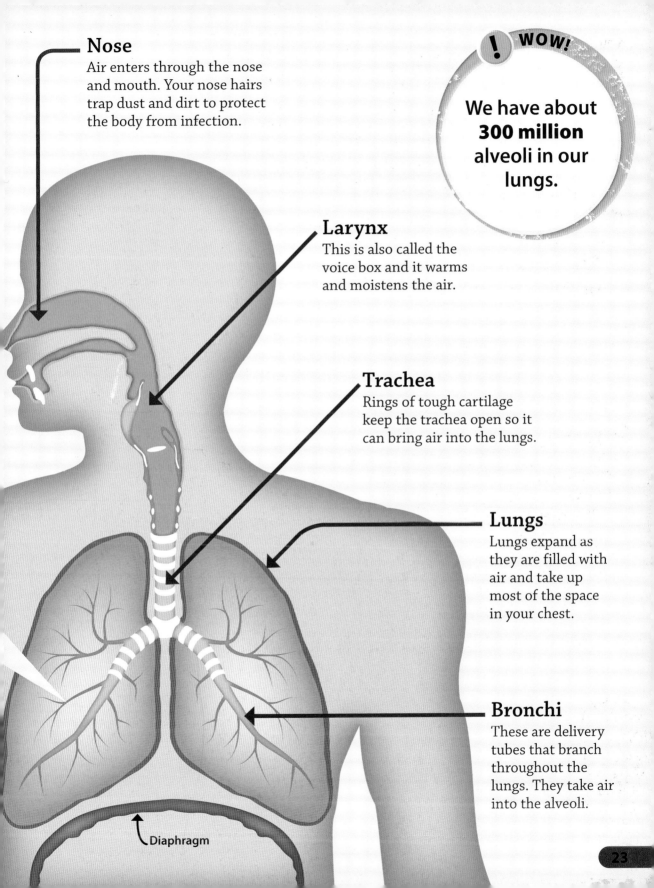

Nose

Air enters through the nose and mouth. Your nose hairs trap dust and dirt to protect the body from infection.

Larynx

This is also called the voice box and it warms and moistens the air.

Trachea

Rings of tough cartilage keep the trachea open so it can bring air into the lungs.

Lungs

Lungs expand as they are filled with air and take up most of the space in your chest.

Bronchi

These are delivery tubes that branch throughout the lungs. They take air into the alveoli.

Diaphragm

Blood

Blood contains a mixture of cells. It has three important jobs as it pulses around the body through blood vessels. The first is to deliver oxygen to body parts so that they can work. It also removes carbon dioxide from body cells and returns it to the lungs to be breathed out. Finally, it fights infection.

Blood types

Your blood is one of four different blood groups. It all depends on the type of antigen (badge) each red blood cell has on its surface. If the antigen is an "A" type, then your blood will be blood group A.

Group O
No antigens on the surface.

Group A
Yellow blobs show the A antigen.

Group B
Blue arrows show the B antigen.

Group AB
This group has both antigens.

Plasma makes up 54 per cent of blood.

Plasma

Gooey plasma is a mixture of water and proteins. The water has salts in it to keep the body working well. The proteins are needed to transport things around the body. Antibodies that fight infection are also found in plasma.

Plasma is lighter than red and white blood cells.

White blood cells

White blood cells are like little soldiers who fight against bacteria and viruses that enter the body. There are many different types of white blood cell, each with their own job to do.

White blood cells and platelets make up one per cent of blood.

Platelets

When a part of the body is cut and starts bleeding, platelets rush to help. They bind together to form a plug to stop the bleeding.

These tiny cells can fit through small spaces.

Red blood cells

Red blood cells make blood red. They get their colour from a substance called haemoglobin (hee-mo-GLO-bin), which carries oxygen and carbon dioxide around the body.

Red blood cells make up 45 per cent of blood.

Immune squad

Cells in your blood are constantly on the lookout for danger. Invaders can enter your body through the air or cut skin. White blood cells are the tiny superheroes that fight them off! They are part of your immune system, which keeps you healthy.

White blood cells work in teams. There is a patrol team, a messenger team, and a stealth team. They're always ready to spring into action!

Patrol team

Messenger team

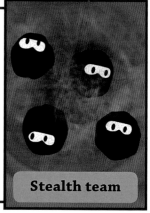

Stealth team

The patrol team wander around your body, making sure everything is in order. They look out for invaders called bacteria and viruses.

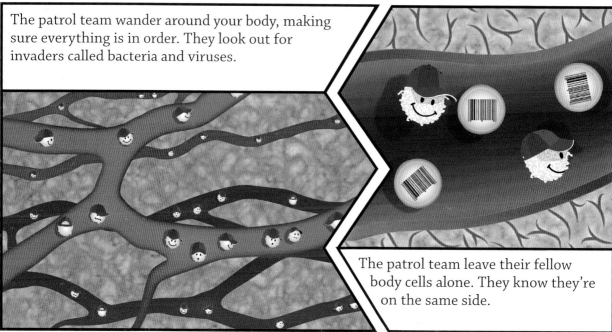

The patrol team leave their fellow body cells alone. They know they're on the same side.

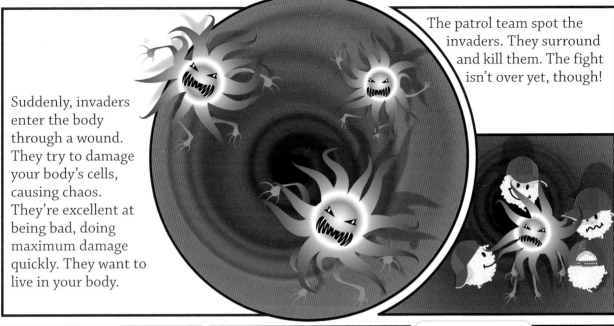

Suddenly, invaders enter the body through a wound. They try to damage your body's cells, causing chaos. They're excellent at being bad, doing maximum damage quickly. They want to live in your body.

The patrol team spot the invaders. They surround and kill them. The fight isn't over yet, though!

We need help!

We'll get the stealth team!

There are too many invaders to battle! Messengers run to get help from the stealth team. They tell the stealth team what weapons to bring.

Good work!

The stealth team make thousands of copies of themselves. An entire army is formed. They defeat the invaders!

We'll be ready next time!

We'll be back!

Some of the stealth team become memory cells, who remember the invaders. If the same invader tries to strike again, the stealth team will be ready...

Healing

Your amazing body has ways of checking to see if everything is healthy or not. Healing is when the body repairs itself to become healthy again. We have armies of repair cells that spring into action whenever something goes wrong. Their job is to patch us up again!

Blood clotting

When you cut yourself, blood cells stick together to form a plug called a clot. This stops you from losing a lot of blood.

Bone fixing

The body mends broken bones by knitting the broken bits together. If the break is really big, doctors will use pins to join the bones.

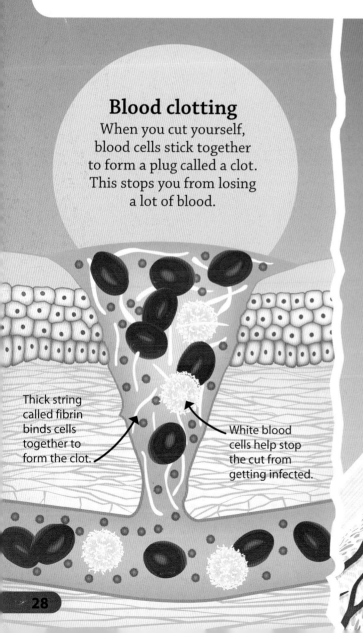

Thick string called fibrin binds cells together to form the clot.

White blood cells help stop the cut from getting infected.

Bone cells make new bone to help with the healing.

New skin

The top layer of your skin is replaced every month. When you cut your skin, the body has repair cells that can quickly stop the bleeding and make brand new skin.

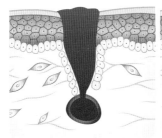
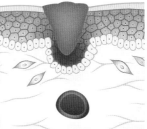
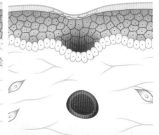

Cut skin bleeds
Blood escapes from the damaged blood vessels on to the skin.

Blood clots
Blood clots to form a scab and stop the bleeding. Repair cells start working.

New skin forms
Repair cells make new skin to close the gap.

Brain mending

Neurones (brain cells) work together to perform brain activity. They are constantly making new connections with each other. If the brain is injured, they repair things.

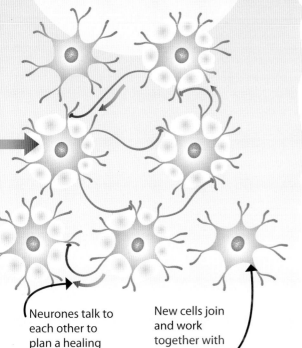

Neurones talk to each other to plan a healing response.

New cells join and work together with the neurones.

Sleep!

During sleep, the body gets to work repairing muscle, filing away memories, and setting the body up for the next day. This is the ultimate healing process.

Digestion

Food doesn't just taste nice, it keeps your body working. Bodies can only use food broken down into its smallest form. This process is called digestion. Food is mashed up in organs such as the stomach, before the intestines soak up the useful parts.

Fibre

The bits of the food we can't use, like fibre, go through the intestines and pass out of the body as poo. Though we can't digest fibres, it's important to eat them to help keep the intestines healthy.

High-fibre foods

Looking inside

Doctors can see inside you to check you're healthy. This tiny camera can be swallowed and takes pictures as it moves through the intestines.

Pill camera

! WOW!

Our intestines are **6.5 m (21 ft)** long, which is nearly as long as **a bus!**

1

Mouth

When you chew, your teeth break down the food into smaller parts before you can swallow it.

2

Oesophagus

This is the food pipe. Food is squeezed through this pipe to land in the stomach.

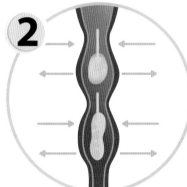

3

Stomach

The stomach blends food into pulp. It has strong acid in it that helps dissolve the food and kills bacteria.

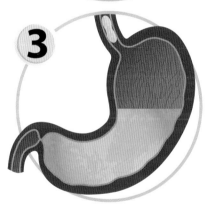

4

Intestines

These soak up bits of the food the body can use. The parts of the food that can't be used are made into poo.

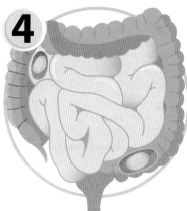

Getting energy

We eat food to give us energy to do things like running about. Even thinking needs lots of energy! Nutrients are the goodness found in different foods. It's important to eat more of what's in the big circles on this page, and less of the food in the smaller circles, to keep your body healthy.

Cholesterol

Cholesterol is a type of fat that helps our cells to work and keep healthy. You shouldn't eat too much of this!

Eggs

Red meat

Red cabbage

Oranges

Broccoli

Vitamins

The body needs vitamins to prevent infections and help build and repair body cells. Fresh fruit and vegetables have lots of vitamins.

Pineapple

Bell peppers

Strawberries

70%
of your body is made up of water.

Candy canes

Sugars

Sugars give us short bursts of energy and should only be eaten in small amounts.

Cupcakes

Chocolate cake

Water

It's important to drink lots of water. Water is needed to keep all your cells working properly. Food has some water, too.

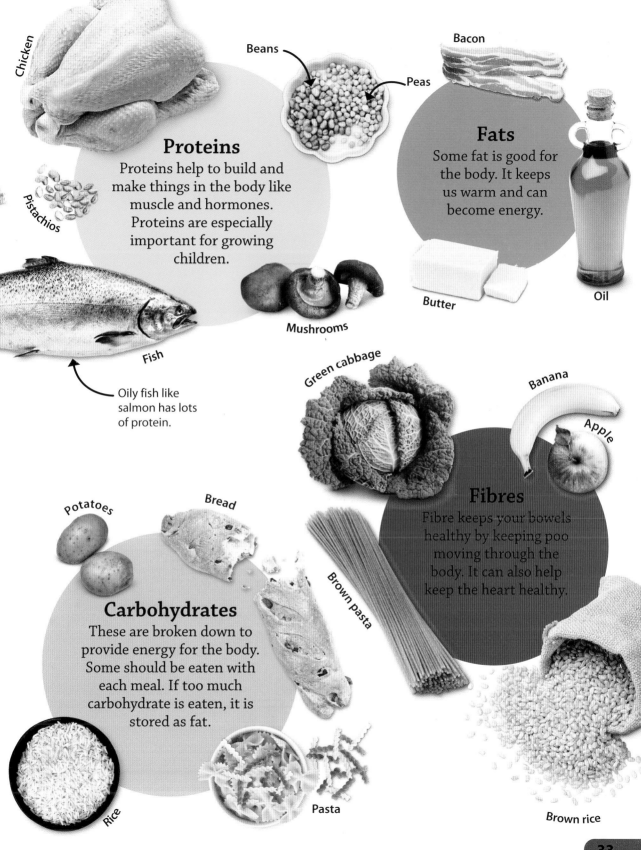

Chicken

Beans

Peas

Bacon

Proteins

Proteins help to build and make things in the body like muscle and hormones. Proteins are especially important for growing children.

Fats

Some fat is good for the body. It keeps us warm and can become energy.

Pistachios

Butter

Oil

Fish

Oily fish like salmon has lots of protein.

Mushrooms

Green cabbage

Banana

Apple

Fibres

Fibre keeps your bowels healthy by keeping poo moving through the body. It can also help keep the heart healthy.

Potatoes

Bread

Brown pasta

Carbohydrates

These are broken down to provide energy for the body. Some should be eaten with each meal. If too much carbohydrate is eaten, it is stored as fat.

Rice

Pasta

Brown rice

Teeth

Teeth help break down the food we eat so that it can be swallowed safely. Saliva is the fluid produced when you eat or even think about food. It keeps the teeth healthy by making acids in everyday food less acidic. Acids would damage your teeth otherwise! Without a full set of teeth, it would be hard to speak properly. Your tongue uses teeth to make sounds like "t".

Keep them clean
Tiny bacteria stick to teeth after you eat food. Brushing twice a day gets rid of them.

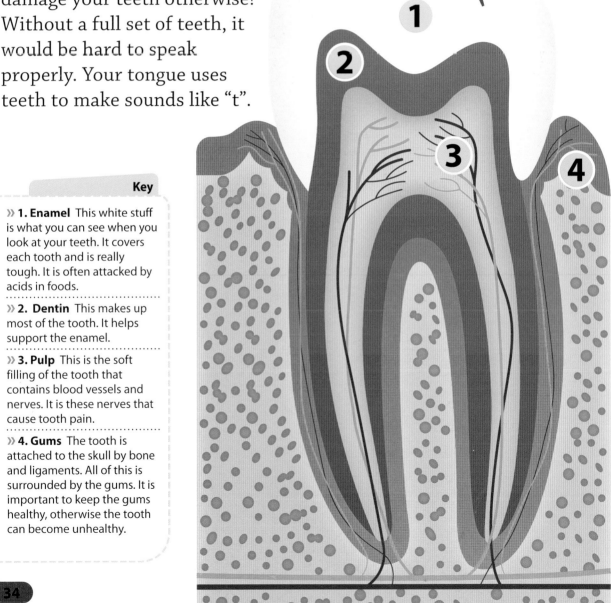

Key

» **1. Enamel** This white stuff is what you can see when you look at your teeth. It covers each tooth and is really tough. It is often attacked by acids in foods.

» **2. Dentin** This makes up most of the tooth. It helps support the enamel.

» **3. Pulp** This is the soft filling of the tooth that contains blood vessels and nerves. It is these nerves that cause tooth pain.

» **4. Gums** The tooth is attached to the skull by bone and ligaments. All of this is surrounded by the gums. It is important to keep the gums healthy, otherwise the tooth can become unhealthy.

Child to adult teeth

Teeth grow inside the gums and push their way out. Children have 20 teeth by around the age of three. These start to fall out at the age of five or six, when adult teeth push them out of their place.

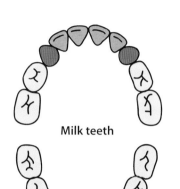

Milk teeth

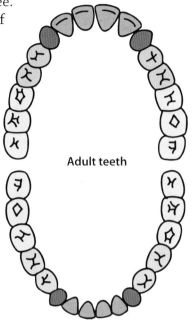

Adult teeth

■ Incisors

■ Canines

■ Premolars

■ Molars

Different jobs

Teeth come in different shapes and sizes. Each type of tooth has a special job to help you eat your food. We go through childhood without premolars!

Premolar
These don't appear until about the age of ten. They have two points for tearing, and a flat part for crushing.

Canine
These teeth are sharp and pointy, and are used for tearing mouthfuls off a larger piece of food.

Incisor
These are right at the front of your mouth. They are used for chopping up food into smaller pieces.

Molar
These are the biggest teeth, right at the back. They crush and grind food just before you swallow it.

The body clock

This clock is in charge of telling your body what to do at different times of the day and night. Part of the brain controls the body clock. These different activities are called circadian rhythms. They are affected by the environment, such as the amount of daylight there is, as well as your genes.

06:00–08:59 pm

03:00–05:59 pm

12:00–02:59 pm

Feeling sleepy
Melatonin is a hormone that makes you sleepy. We produce lots of it when it gets dark outside.

Get active!
Your body temperature has warmed up through the day and is now perfect for exercising. The organs are ready for a workout.

Body napping
You've just had lunch. Blood rushes to your stomach to digest food. The rest of the body and the brain relaxes a bit.

09:00 pm–05:59 am

Fast asleep
High levels of melatonin keep us asleep. The brain files away memories and the body repairs itself for the next day.

Artificial light
Light from electronic devices such as phones tricks the brain into thinking it's time to wake up. It's best not to use them before bed.

06:00–08:59 am

Wake up!
We stop producing melatonin in the morning. We stop feeling sleepy and are wide awake, ready to face the day!

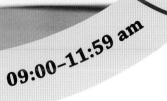

09:00–11:59 am

Concentration time
Cortisol (a hormone) makes us feel alert. The body makes cortisol overnight, which means you work best in the morning!

Genes

What colour is your hair? What colour are your eyes? It's your genes that decide! They have been passed down through your family. Genes contain information about what we look like and behave like. Genes are in every one of your cells.

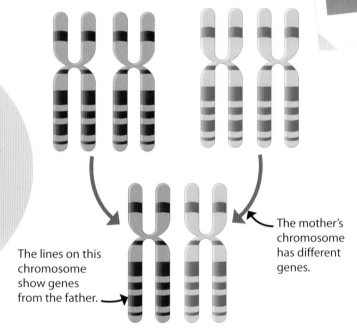

Freckles are patches of colour on the skin.

The lines on this chromosome show genes from the father.

The mother's chromosome has different genes.

Gene carriers

Genes are found on chromosomes inside your cells. We have 23 pairs of chromosomes. One chromosome of each pair is from our mother and one is from our father. Children look like a combination of their parents because they have genes from their mother and father.

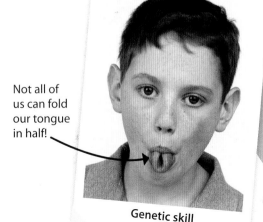

Not all of us can fold our tongue in half!

Genetic skill

Amazing abilities

Our genes control what we can do. Some people can roll their tongue and some can't. If you can roll your tongue, it's because your genes have instructions on how to do this.

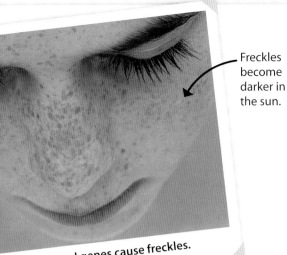

Freckles become darker in the sun.

Sunshine and genes cause freckles.

Strong and weak

Strong genes rule over weak genes. The colour of your eyes is controlled by genes. Brown-eyed genes (B) are strong and blue-eyed genes (b) are weak. If someone inherits both brown and blue, the strong brown will win! However, their child could still have blue eyes if the weak blue gene is passed on.

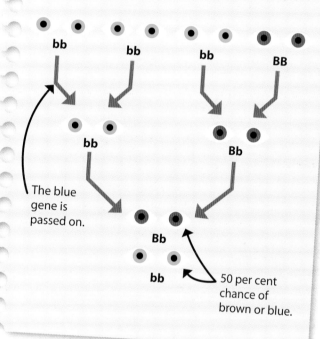

bb

bb

bb

BB

bb

Bb

The blue gene is passed on.

Bb

bb

50 per cent chance of brown or blue.

Genes or environment?

Some physical features are mainly controlled by environmental factors from the world around us, others mainly by genes, and some by both, such as weight.

This ladder is folded up and lives in the cell's nucleus.

DNA

Genes are made of DNA, which looks like a really long ladder. It is full of information and is found inside our cells. DNA provides instructions to cells on how to do their jobs to keep the body working.

! **WOW!**

We have about **2,000 genes in our bodies!**

Senses

We experience the world around us through our senses. Tiny points around our bodies called sensory receptors collect information about the world outside. This keeps the body safe. It also keeps things such as temperature at the right level, so the body can work properly. Special senses such as sight use a whole organ to gather information.

Sensory receptors

These points around the body gather different information. When you feel hot, your temperature receptors detect this. They send information to the brain, which tells you to take your jumper off so you don't overheat!

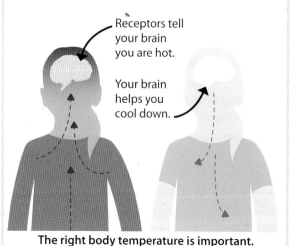

Receptors tell your brain you are hot.

Your brain helps you cool down.

The right body temperature is important.

Sound

Hearing is a special sense. It helps us communicate with others. Listening to sounds helps us to stay safe. When you hear a car coming, you know not to cross the road.

TEMPERATURE

We can find out how hot or cold something is just by touching it. The temperature receptors in our hands tell us this information.

Pressure

Pressure receptors tell us how hard to grip things. Pressure receptors in the fingers tell you how hard to hold things so they don't get damaged.

TASTE

Taste is a special sense. Taste buds detect different types of taste, telling you if the food you're eating is sweet or sour.

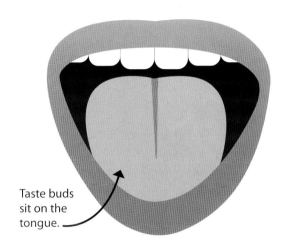

Taste buds sit on the tongue.

Smell

Smell is a special sense. The nose has smell receptors. Food that's gone off smells bad. When you smell it, you don't want to eat it. This protects your body.

Sight

Sight is a special sense with its own organ, the eye. Seeing things with our eyes tells us a lot about the world. It helps us not to walk into things!

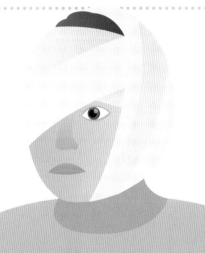

Pain

Feeling pain is not nice, but it keeps our bodies safe. Pain receptors detect the pain and you know not to bump your head again!

Balance

Our sense of balance helps us not to fall over. Having poor balance means we might fall over a lot. Being able to walk in a straight line means you have good balance.

Balance is sensed in the ear.

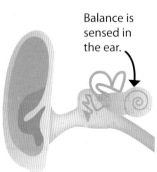

Eyes

Sight enables us to see the world around us. We can see all the colours of the rainbow, as well as black and white, because of our eyes. When you go from a dark room into the sunshine, the eyes adapt so you can see everything.

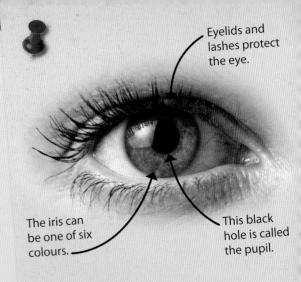

Eyelids and lashes protect the eye.

The iris can be one of six colours.

This black hole is called the pupil.

Parts of the eye

Look in a mirror to identify the different parts of your eye. Your eyelids close to protect the eye from getting scratched.

How it works

We see things clearly when light falls on the retina at the back of the eye. Light is focused onto the retina by the lens. An upside-down image appears there to be taken to the brain and turned the right way up.

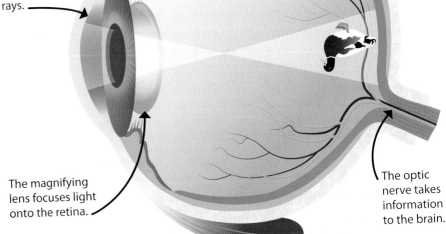

Light receptors in the retina detect sight.

The colourless cornea bends light rays.

Light rays reflect off the duck and enter our eyes.

The magnifying lens focuses light onto the retina.

The optic nerve takes information to the brain.

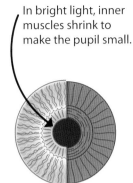

In bright light, inner muscles shrink to make the pupil small.

In the dark, outer muscles shrink to make the pupil big.

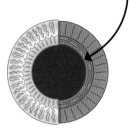

Changing size

The iris has muscles to change the size of the pupil in different light. A bigger pupil lets in more light in the dark to help us see.

Light hits retina.

Light doesn't hit retina properly.

Seeing clearly

The shape of your eyeballs affects how well you can see. If an eye is too long, light doesn't hit the retina properly. This means you're short sighted. Glasses help you see clearly.

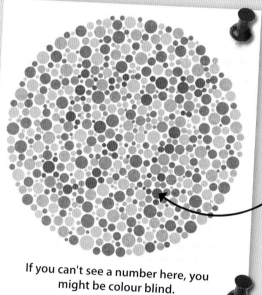

Tiny cones at the back of the eye help us see red and green.

If you can't see a number here, you might be colour blind.

Colour blindness

Colour blindness is when someone can't see a particular colour or isn't able to tell the difference between two colours.

! WOW!

The **eye** is mostly made up of **jelly** called **vitreous humour.**

Hearing

The ears collect all sorts of information about the sounds we hear every day. Sounds can be loud or soft, high or low. Each of our voices has a different sound. Our maze-like ears and brilliant brain work together to tell us whose voice we are listening to. Hearing helps us work out what is going on around us.

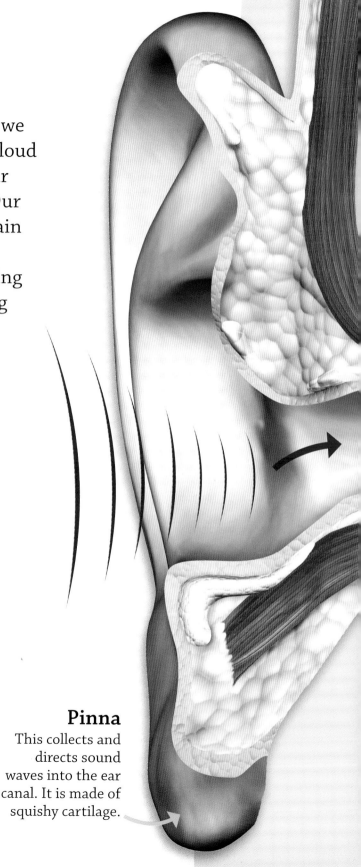

Sorting out sound

Information about how loud sounds are and where they are coming from is taken to both sides of the brain. The information travels up the vestibulocochlear (vest-ee-boo-lock-ock-lee-ar) nerves that run from each ear.

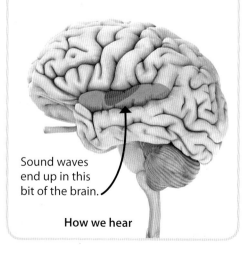

Sound waves end up in this bit of the brain.

How we hear

Pinna
This collects and directs sound waves into the ear canal. It is made of squishy cartilage.

Ears help you keep your **balance** as well as **hear!**

Vestibulocochlear nerve

Nerves carry information to the brain. This nerve takes sound to the brain, which tells you what you're hearing.

Middle ear bones

The malleus, incus, and stapes are bones in your ear that shake when the ear drum vibrates.

Ear canal

This tube transfers sound to the ear drum. It should contain wax, which keeps it healthy.

Ear drum

This is a thin sheet of tissue that vibrates when sound hits it.

Cochlea

This processes the sound and also helps with balance. It looks like a snail!

Auditory tube

This secret passageway from the ear to the throat helps stop ear pressure building up.

Taste and smell

These two senses are closely linked together. If you have a blocked nose, you might not be able to taste food because smell helps you taste. Bad tastes and smells keep us safe from eating things that might harm us, like rotten food. Children have more taste buds than adults, which makes them like sweeter foods!

Taste buds have nerves that tell our brain about the flavour of food.

Taste buds
You have tiny bumps on the surface of your tongue that can be seen in the mirror. These are taste buds (papillae), which help us to taste different foods.

Sour lemon

Types of taste
The four main tastes are sweet, salty, bitter, and sour. A newly named fifth taste called umami is savoury, like the taste of tomatoes or soy sauce.

REALLY?

! **80 per cent** of a food's **flavour** comes from its **smell!**

Sweet chocolate

Salty seaweed

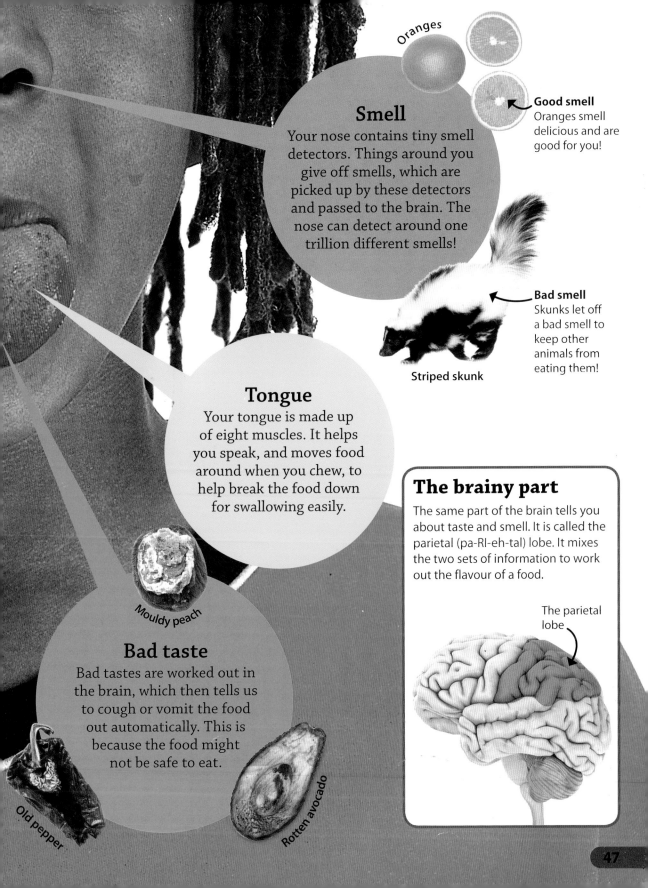

Smell

Your nose contains tiny smell detectors. Things around you give off smells, which are picked up by these detectors and passed to the brain. The nose can detect around one trillion different smells!

Oranges

Good smell
Oranges smell delicious and are good for you!

Bad smell
Skunks let off a bad smell to keep other animals from eating them!

Striped skunk

Tongue

Your tongue is made up of eight muscles. It helps you speak, and moves food around when you chew, to help break the food down for swallowing easily.

The brainy part

The same part of the brain tells you about taste and smell. It is called the parietal (pa-RI-eh-tal) lobe. It mixes the two sets of information to work out the flavour of a food.

The parietal lobe

Mouldy peach

Bad taste

Bad tastes are worked out in the brain, which then tells us to cough or vomit the food out automatically. This is because the food might not be safe to eat.

Old pepper

Rotten avocado

Emotions

Emotions are what we feel. When you see your friends you feel happy, but a tiger would probably make you feel scared! Feeling happy, sad, worried, and scared are all emotions. Some emotions are there to help us survive. Feeling scared of a tiger stops you from going near it.

Angry
You might feel angry if you can't do something, or if someone is mean to you.

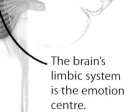

The brain's limbic system is the emotion centre.

Inside your head
The brain tells us how we feel and how to react. Remembering how something makes us feel helps us know whether to do it again or not.

Happy
Feeling happy can make us want to repeat useful actions – for example, doing well in a test.

Your feelings
It's normal to feel sad or angry sometimes, but happiness is most people's favourite emotion. Certain activities can help you feel happier.

Talking about feelings.

Spending time with friends.

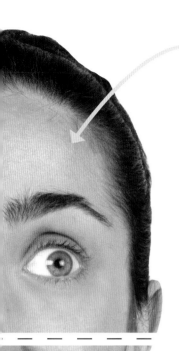

Scared

When you've done something wrong, you might be scared of getting told off!

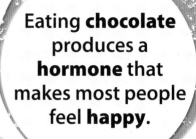

!

Eating **chocolate** produces a **hormone** that makes most people feel **happy**.

Adrenaline travels around the body.

Adrenaline

When you are scared, your body releases a hormone called adrenaline. It tells the heart and other body parts to work harder so that you can run away.

Sad

We might feel sad when something important changes in our life. Sadness usually only lasts a short time!

Spiders often make people feel scared.

Eating healthy food.

Doing exercise such as sports.

Skin bacteria

Many types of tiny living things called bacteria live on our skin. They form a community to help keep us healthy. They make sure the skin is protected against invasion by harmful bugs. Different parts of the skin are suited to different bacteria.

! **WOW!**

There are around **1000** different types of **bacteria** living on your skin!

Staphylococcus epidermidis

Forearm
Micrococci are really tough. They are happy to live in dry conditions, like on your forearm. They also like a lot of salt! This makes the skin a good home for them.

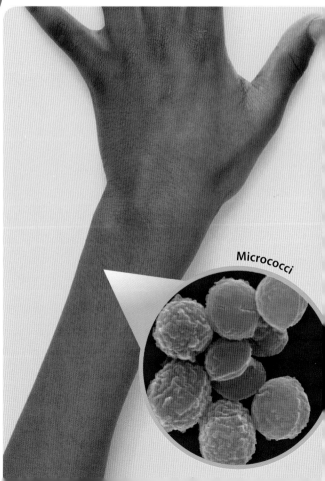

Micrococci

Hands
Bacteria are found all over the body and especially on the hands. They help keep the skin healthy. Bacteria that permanently live on the skin are called resident bacteria. Bacteria that visit the skin are called transient.

Keeping clean

Being clean helps us stay healthy. We pick up bacteria throughout the day. There are some basic things you can do to keep clean so that nasty bacteria don't make their home on your body.

Wash your hands after going to the toilet.

Have a shower or bath every day.

Brush your teeth twice a day.

Corynebacterium

Nose
Lots of good bacteria live in the nose. They protect against invasion by bad bacteria. Staphylococcus aureus lives in the nose. It can cause nasty diseases in the lungs if it takes over the good bacteria.

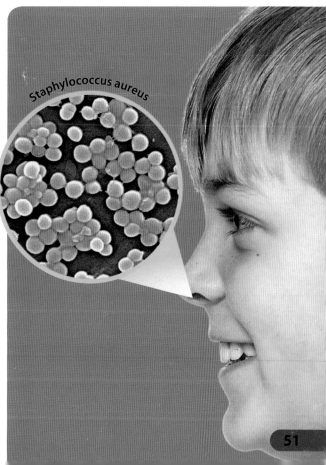

Staphylococcus aureus

Armpit
Sweat glands under the armpit make sticky sweat, which acts as food for bacteria. When you reach your teens, your sweat starts to smell. It's the bacteria that munches on the sweat that makes it smelly!

E.COLI BACTERIA

» **Size:** Ten times thinner than a sheet of paper.

» **How you get infected:** Eating food that has gone off or not been cooked properly.

» **Symptoms:** Stomach cramps, runny poo, high temperature, and feeling generally unwell.

» **Treatment:** Drink lots of water and rest at home.

» **How to avoid it:** Wash hands regularly with soap and water, especially after using the toilet.

Bacteria...

An infection is when tiny living things called pathogens invade the body to upset it. Pathogens can be bacteria or viruses. They work in different ways to make us ill.

Antibiotics

Antibiotics enter the bacteria to stop it from working properly. This causes the bacteria to die. Antibiotics only work if the infection is caused by bacteria.

Bacteria

Good bacteria help us stay healthy. Bad bacteria can make their home in our bodies and produce poisons called toxins. These stop the healthy cells from working properly. Bacteria drain the body's energy, making you feel tired.

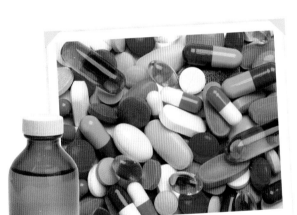

Each antibiotic kills different bacteria.

Some bacteria have tails to help them move about.

Around a spoonful of liquid antibiotics is needed at a time.

! REALLY?

Superbugs are bacteria that can no longer be **killed** by antibiotics.

or virus?

The pathogens try to take over the body. They produce poisons to kill the body's cells. Our bodies fight back. This battle makes us feel poorly.

FLU VIRUS

» **Size:** Three million times smaller than a drop of water.

» **How you get infected:** By breathing it in the air, usually after someone has sneezed.

» **Symptoms:** High temperature, cough, tiredness, runny nose, and achey body.

» **Treatment:** Drink plenty of water and rest. Keep eating healthily.

» **How to avoid it:** Cough or sneeze into a tissue then throw it away. Wash your hands regularly.

Ahh choo!

Nasty viruses that cause colds make you sneeze. We sneeze to keep harmful things out of the nose.

Viruses infect the body cell and change the way it works.

Virus

Viruses must get inside a cell before they can start working. Once inside, they multiply and change the cell. This causes us to be ill.

Vaccines

These are injected into the body to stop viruses from living inside us. Vaccines contain a small amount of the virus, but not enough to cause problems.

The body finds the vaccine's virus and starts to fight it. The body produces memory cells.

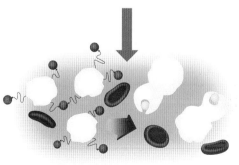

If the same virus invades the body again, the memory cells kill it off quickly.

Exercise

Exercise is good for the whole body. It keeps the organs working properly. It makes bones and muscles stronger. It also makes you feel happier. We were built to move around a lot rather than sit down for hours. Exercise has lots of effects on the body!

Blood vessels
These get bigger so heat can escape.

2

Red face

The heart pumps blood around the body quickly, and muscles make heat as they work. To stop you getting too hot, blood vessels get bigger. This makes you go bright red!

Lungs
More oxygen from the air is needed by the body.

1

Respiratory system

You breathe harder and faster when you exercise. The lungs work hard to get oxygen to your organs and to remove carbon dioxide from them.

Drink water
You sweat out water so remember to replace it!

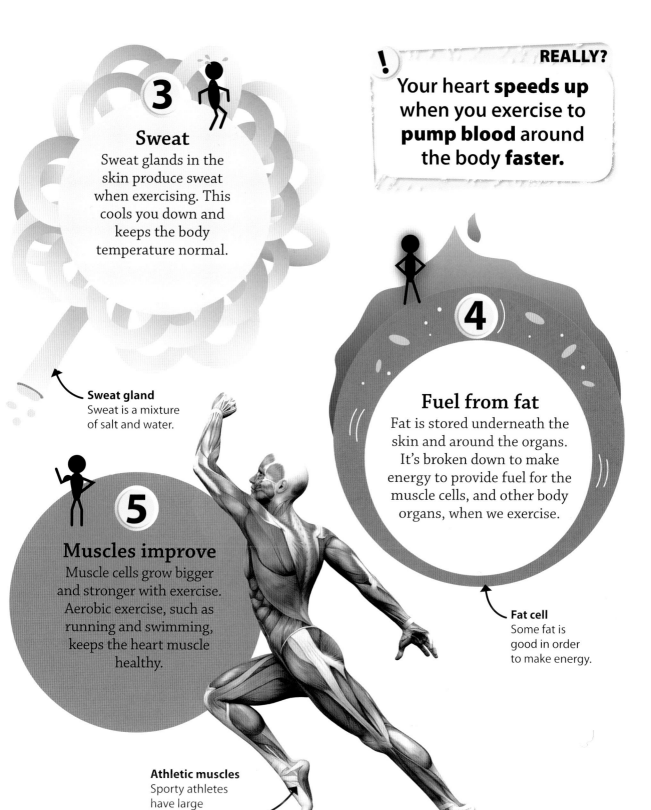

3
Sweat
Sweat glands in the skin produce sweat when exercising. This cools you down and keeps the body temperature normal.

REALLY?
Your heart **speeds up** when you exercise to **pump blood** around the body **faster.**

Sweat gland
Sweat is a mixture of salt and water.

4
Fuel from fat
Fat is stored underneath the skin and around the organs. It's broken down to make energy to provide fuel for the muscle cells, and other body organs, when we exercise.

Fat cell
Some fat is good in order to make energy.

5
Muscles improve
Muscle cells grow bigger and stronger with exercise. Aerobic exercise, such as running and swimming, keeps the heart muscle healthy.

Athletic muscles
Sporty athletes have large muscles.

Arm

3D machines can scan an arm and print a new one using special material. The printers can add real body cells to the arm!

3D-printed arm

Hip

If the hip joint breaks, doctors take out the broken bits and replace them with metal. Lots of people have metal hip joints.

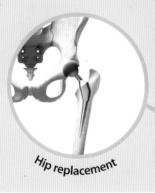

Hip replacement

Superhuman

Scientists can make artificial body parts to replace parts that are missing or not working. These look and work like the real thing. Some man-made limbs can even be controlled by the brain!

Knee

Knee bones rub together a lot and can wear down, causing pain. The bones can be replaced with a metal joint. This takes the pain away.

Knee replacement

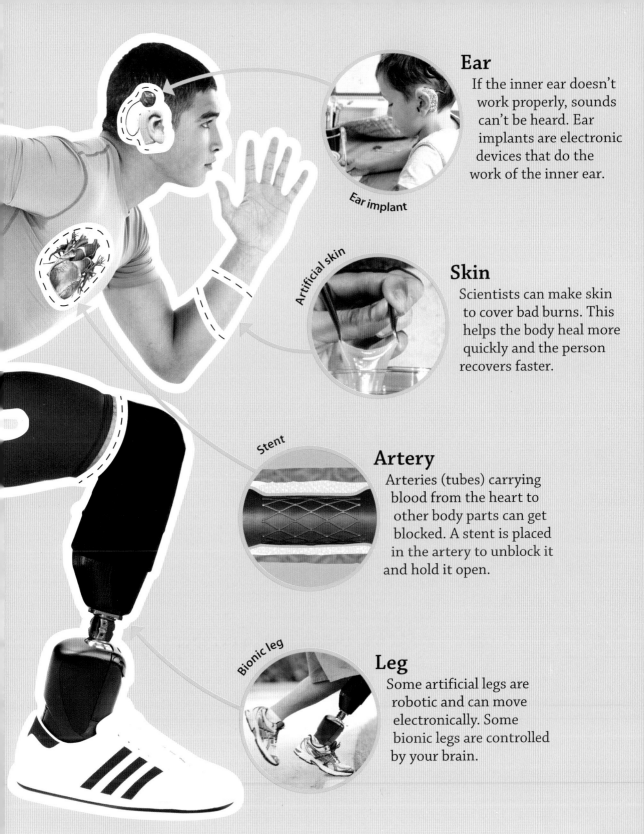

Ear

If the inner ear doesn't work properly, sounds can't be heard. Ear implants are electronic devices that do the work of the inner ear.

Ear implant

Artificial skin

Skin

Scientists can make skin to cover bad burns. This helps the body heal more quickly and the person recovers faster.

Stent

Artery

Arteries (tubes) carrying blood from the heart to other body parts can get blocked. A stent is placed in the artery to unblock it and hold it open.

Bionic leg

Leg

Some artificial legs are robotic and can move electronically. Some bionic legs are controlled by your brain.

Human body facts and figures

The human body is more complex than our entire planet! Here are some amazing facts about your body, and what it can do.

Gastric juice released by the stomach is so **acidic** it can **dissolve metal**.

Gooey gastric juice helps to kill germs and digest food.

Brains are about 75 per cent water!

Bone is **six times stronger** than the same weight of **steel**!

60 KM

(37 miles)
The total length of nerves in the body is 60 km (37 miles).

250 MILLION
A single drop of blood contains around 250 million red blood cells, and 275,000 white blood cells!

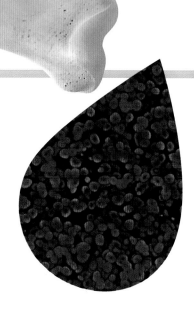

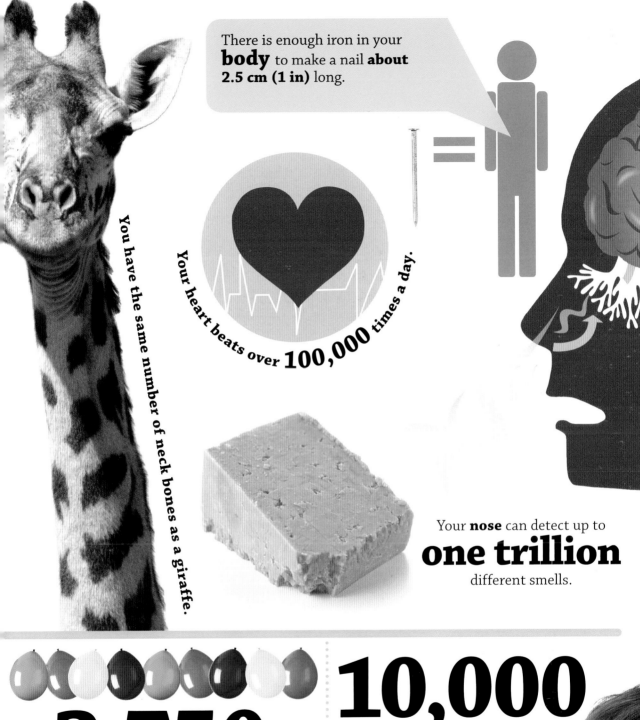

There is enough iron in your **body** to make a nail **about 2.5 cm (1 in)** long.

You have the same number of neck bones as a giraffe.

Your heart beats over **100,000** times a day.

Your **nose** can detect up to **one trillion** different smells.

3,750

You breathe out enough air in one day to inflate around 3,750 balloons!

10,000

You blink your eyelids around 10,000 times a day, shutting out dust to help keep your eyes squeaky clean.

Glossary

Here are the meanings of some words that are useful for you to know when learning all about the human body.

acid Liquid that can dissolve things

artery Tube that carries blood around the body from the heart

bacteria Tiny living things that can live on the skin and inside the body

blood Liquid that carries cells with different jobs

blood vessel Tube that carries blood around the body

bone Part of the structure of the body that gives support and protects organs

bowels Another word for intestines, these organs take goodness from food for the body to use and get rid of waste

brain Control centre of the body that tells it what to do and works out what we sense and how we feel

breathing Taking in oxygen to keep the body's cells working

carbon dioxide Gas made by body cells that can't be used by the body

cartilage Soft material used in the structure of the body

cell Tiny parts of the body that carry out different jobs, such as fighting infection

digestion Process of breaking down food to be used by the body

disease Problem that means the body can't work properly

DNA Chemical that genes are made of

doctor Person trained to heal people who are ill or injured

electrical connection Things joined by a type of energy called electricity

energy Force that allows things to keep working

environment Things around us or inside us

fat Material in the body used to store energy

genes Sections of DNA that carry instructions for how the body looks

germs Bacteria or viruses

glands Parts of the body that make different chemicals

healthy Working properly

heart Organ that pumps blood around the body

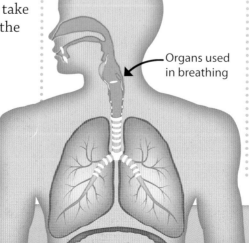

Organs used in breathing

hormone Chemical messenger that tell the body what to do

immune system Parts of the body that work together to fight infection

infection Virus or a type of bacteria that gets inside the body and causes harm

injection Using a needle to transfer liquid such as a vaccine into someone's body

ligament Material that holds bones together

medicine Liquid or pill used to fix the body if it isn't working properly

memory Something from the past that is kept inside the mind

muscle Material in the body that contracts (shortens) to allow movement

nerve "Wire" that carries information between the brain and body

neurone Brain cell

nucleus Part of the cell that tells it what to do

organ Part of the body made of tissue that does a particular job, such as the heart

oxygen Gas that allows every part of the body to keep working

process Series of actions that are carried out to do a job, such as breathing

protein Part of a cell that affects how the cell does its job, or a type of food that helps build a healthy body

receptor Part of the body that picks up information

respiratory To do with breathing

sense Information that tells us about our environment, such as sight

sensor Part of the body that picks up information from the surroundings

sensory Involving a sense, such as hearing

skeleton Structure of bones that make up the body

skin Organ that covers the body

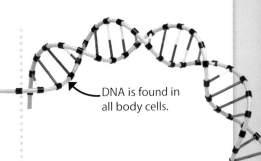

DNA is found in all body cells.

spine Column of bones in the back protecting the spinal cord

structure Something usually made up of different parts

surgery Mending something inside a patient that isn't working properly

system Body parts that work together to perform a job, such as digestion

tissue Material in the body made up of similar cells

vaccine Injection that teaches the body how to fight an infection

vein Tube that carries blood from the body to the heart

virus Tiny thing from outside the body that invades the body's cells

womb Part of the female body where babies grow

Index

A

acid 19, 31, 34, 58, 60
adrenaline 49
alveoli 22
antibiotics 52
antigens 24
arteries 21, 57, 60
artificial legs 57
asthma 22
atria 20

B

babies 6, 11
bacteria 25, 26–27, 34, 50–51, 52, 60
balance 41, 45
bionic limbs 57
blood 8, 20–21, 22, 24–25, 58, 60
blood clots 28, 29
blood vessels 11, 20–21, 24, 29, 54, 60
body clock 36–37
bone marrow 8
bones 4, 6–11, 28, 54, 55, 58, 60
bowels 4, 19, 60
brain 4, 10, 11, 12–15, 19, 29, 36, 44, 47, 48, 58, 60
breathing 22–23, 59, 60
bronchi 23

C

carbohydrates 33
carbon dioxide 20, 22, 24, 25, 60
cartilage 8, 60

cells 4, 5, 12, 22, 26, 27, 38, 60
children 6, 11, 35, 46
cholesterol 32
chromosomes 38
cochlea 45
colour blindness 43
cornea 42
cranium 11

D

digestive system 5, 30–31, 60
diseases 53, 60
DNA 38, 60
doctors 30, 60

E

ears 11, 12, 40, 44–45, 57
ear canal 45
ear drum 45
electrical connections 12, 14, 19, 60
embryo 6
emotions 48–49
enamel 34, 35
energy 32, 55, 60
environment 36, 60
exercise 54–55
eyes 11, 13, 38, 39, 41, 42–43, 59

F

fat 32, 33, 55, 60
feelings 48–49
fetus 6
fibre 30, 33
food 30–33, 41, 46

freckles 38, 39
frontal lobe 12, 13

G

genes 38–39, 60
germs 26–27, 52–53, 60
glands 51, 60
glasses 43
growth 6–7
gums 34

H

hair 38
hands 7, 50
healing 28–29
hearing 11, 12, 44–45, 57
heart 4, 13, 17, 20–21, 54, 55, 57, 59, 60
hip replacements 56
hormones 7, 36, 37, 49, 60

I

immune system 26–27, 61
incisors 35
infections 52–53, 61
injections 53, 61
intestines 16, 30–31, 60
iris 42, 43

J

jaw 10, 11
joints 9

K

kidneys 4, 19
knee 7, 56

L

larynx 23
legs 7, 16–17, 57
lens 42
ligaments 9, 61
liver 4, 19
lungs 19, 22–23, 54

M

medicine 61
melatonin 37
membrane, cell 5
memory 12, 61
milk teeth 35
molars 35
motor cortex 13
mouth 31, 35
movement 13, 14, 54–55
muscles 4, 8, 13, 14, 16–17,
    43, 54, 55, 61

N

nerves 11, 14–15, 42, 45, 58,
    61
nervous system 14–15
neurones 29, 61
neurotransmitters 14
nose 19, 23, 41, 46, 47, 51, 59
nucleus, cell 5, 61

O

oesophagus 31
organ systems 5
organs 4, 18–19, 54, 61
oxygen 20, 22, 24, 25, 54,
    60, 61

P

pain 15, 41
pancreas 19
pathogens 52–53

pill cameras 30
plasma 24
platelets 25
poo 30, 33
premolars 35
pressure receptors 40
processes 61
proteins 24, 33, 61

R

receptors 15, 40, 42, 61
red blood cells 8, 22, 24, 25, 58
respiratory system 22–23,
    54, 61
retina 42

S

saliva 34
seeing 13, 41, 42–43
senses 13, 40–47, 61
sensory receptors 15, 40, 61
skeleton 8–9, 61
skin 4, 18, 29, 50–51, 57, 61
skull 10–11
sleep 29, 36, 37
smell, sense of 13, 41, 46–47,
    59
spatial awareness 12
spinal cord 8, 13, 14
spine 8, 61
stents 57
stomach 19, 30–31, 58
sugars 32
superbugs 52
surgery 56, 61
swallowing 31, 35, 47
sweat 50, 54, 55

T

taste 41, 46–47
taste buds 46

teeth 10–11, 31, 34–35
temperature 36, 40, 55
3D printing 56
tissues 4, 61
tongue 41, 46, 47
trachea 23
transplants 18

U

umami 46

V

vaccines 53, 61
veins 21, 61
ventricles 21
viruses 25, 26–27, 53, 61
vitamins 32

W

water, drinking 32
white blood cells 25, 26–27, 58
womb 61
wounds 27, 28–29

X

X-rays 8

Acknowledgements

The publisher would like to thank the following people for their assistance in the preparation of this book: Dheeraj Arora for additional jacket design; Dan Crisp, Mark Clifton, and Bettina Myklebust Stovne for illustrations; Caroline Hunt for proofreading; Hilary Bird for indexing; Dr. Ruth Grady, Dr. Kathleen Nolan, Dr. David Hughes, Dr. Christian Heintzen, Emma Beacom, and Laurence Cheeseman for consulting.

The publisher would like to thank the following for their kind permission to reproduce their photographs:

(Key: a-above; b-below/bottom; c-centre; f-far; l-left; r-right; t-top)

2 Dorling Kindersley: Arran Lewis (bl). 3 123RF.com: newartgraphics (cb). Dorling Kindersley: Arran Lewis (cr). Dreamstime. com: Studio29ro (crb). 6-7 Dorling Kindersley: Arran Lewis (All Skeletons). 6 Dorling Kindersley: Arran Lewis (cb). 7 Dorling Kindersley: Arran Lewis (cra). 8 Fotolia: Dario Sabljak (tl). Science Photo Library: Microscape (br). 8-9 Dorling Kindersley: Arran Lewis (c). 9 Dorling Kindersley: Arran Lewis (crb). 10 Getty Images: Sciepro (bl). 12 123RF.com: Vitaly Valua / domenicogelermo (c). Fotolia: Cantor Pannatto (br). 13 123RF.com: Jacek Chabraszewski (tl). Dorling Kindersley: The All England Lawn Tennis Club, Church Road, Wimbledon, London (ca). Fotolia: Ramona Heim (cr). 18 Alamy Stock Photo: dpa picture alliance archive (cl). 19 Alamy Stock Photo: leonello calvetti (cr); Friedrich Saurer (tr). 21 Dreamstime.com: Rafael Ben-ari (tr). 24 Science Photo Library: Antonia Reeve (bl). 25 Dreamstime.com: Studio29ro (crb). Science Photo Library: Steve Gschmeissner (tl, c). 30 Alamy Stock Photo: David Bleeker Photography (bc). 32 123RF.com: jessmine (cb); Sergey Mironov / supernam (cra); Viktar Malyshchyts / viktarmalyshchyts (c). 33 123RF. com: amylv (crb). Alamy Stock Photo: Hugh Threlfall (clb). 35 Dorling Kindersley: Arran Lewis (cb). 37 Dreamstime.com: Daniel Jędzura (cra). 39 Dreamstime.com: Marilyn Barbone (tl). 43 123RF.com: Rangizzz (cr). Alamy Stock Photo: Phanie (cl). 47 123RF. com: Eric Isselee (cra). Dorling Kindersley: Stephen Oliver (clb). 50 Getty Images: Media for Medical / Universal Images Group (c). Science Photo Library: Dennis Kunkel

Microscopy (br). 51 Alamy Stock Photo: BSIP SA (cl). Getty Images: BSIP / Universal Images Group (cb). 52 123RF.com: photka (clb). Science Photo Library: Steve Gschmeissner (r). 53 Science Photo Library: Dennis Kunkel Microscopy (l). 54 Dreamstime.com: Akulamatiau (br). 55 123RF.com: newartgraphics (bc). 56 123RF.com: Sebastian Kaulitzki (ca); Tushchakorn Rushchatrabuntchasuk (bc); lightwise (crb). Getty Images: St. Louis Post-Dispatch / Tribune News Service (tc). 57 Alamy Stock Photo: Kathy deWitt (tc); Guido Schiefer (tl). emPOWER™ Ankle image provided with permission of BionX Medical Technologies, Inc.°: (cb). Science Photo Library: H. Raguet / Eurelios (ca). 58 Alamy Stock Photo: CVI Textures (br). 62 Dorling Kindersley: Arran Lewis (tl). 64 123RF.com: newartgraphics (tl)

Cover images: Front: 123RF.com: newartgraphics br; Alamy Stock Photo: l; Dorling Kindersley: Arran Lewis fclb; Back: Alamy Stock Photo: Guido Schiefer cla; Front Flap: 123RF.com: amylv cla, Sebastian Kaulitzki bl; Dreamstime.com: Sam74100 cra; Fotolia: Dario Sabljak cb; Back Flap: Dorling Kindersley: Natural History Museum, London clb, Wardrobe Museum, Salisbury crb; Getty Images: Nash Photos cra; iStockphoto.com: Naumoid ca. Front Endpapers: 123RF.com: David Carillet tc, Sam74100 bc (hands); Alamy Stock Photo: Art Directors & TRIP clb, Photo Researchers, Inc cr; Dorling Kindersley: Thackeray Medical Museum fcra; Getty Images: Science & Society Picture Library cra; iStockphoto.com: Wynnter bc; Wellcome Images http://creativecommons.org/ licenses/by/4.0/: fcl, fcrb, Iconographic Collections c, Rare Books cl, c (Book page); Back Endpapers: 123RF.com: Jovannig c (Fetus), Molekuul tc; Alamy Stock Photo: Marion Kaplan cra, Trinity Mirror / Mirrorpix crb; Dorling Kindersley: Thackeray Medical Museum cla; Getty Images: Alfred Eisenstaedt

/ The LIFE Picture Collection c, Bettmann bl, Karen Bleier / AFP ftr, Mark Runnacles fbr; Science Photo Library: CCI Archives fcla; Wellcome Images http://creativecommons. org/licenses/by/4.0/: Iconographic Collections fcl

All other images © Dorling Kindersley
For further information see:
www.dkimages.com

My Findout facts:

Medical milestones

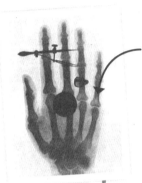

The first X-ray image was of the inventor's wife's hand.

X-ray
German physicist Wilhelm Röntgen invents the first X-ray machine.

Antibiotics
Scottish biologist Alexander Fleming discovers penicillin, the first antibiotic medicine.

Polio vaccine
American virologist Jonas Salk tests first successful vaccine against polio on nearly two million schoolchildren.

Continued from front of book

| 1874 | 1895 | 1901 | 1928 | 1953 | 1954 | 1958 |

DNA
Swiss scientist Johann Miescher discovers DNA.

Structure of DNA
American biologist James Watson and British biologist Francis Crick discover the twisted ladder structure of DNA.

Blood groups
Austrian-American doctor Karl Landsteiner points out the different blood groups.

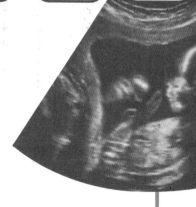

Ultrasound
American doctor Edward Hon and British doctor Ian Donald use ultrasound scanning to look at a fetus inside its mother.